Howling Hurricanes

Louise and Richard Spilsbury

www.heinemann.co.uk/library

Visit our website to find out more information about **Heinemann Library** books.

To order:
☎ Phone 44 (0) 1865 888066
 Send a fax to 44 (0) 1865 314091
💻 Visit the Heinemann Bookshop at www.heinemann.co.uk/library to browse our catalogue and order online.

First published in Great Britain by
Heinemann Library, Halley Court,
Jordan Hill, Oxford OX2 8EJ, part of
Harcourt Education.
Heinemann is a registered trademark of
Harcourt Education Ltd.

Editorial: Andrew Farrow and Dan Nunn
Design: David Poole and Paul Myerscough
Illustrations: Geoff Ward
Picture Research: Rebecca Sodergren and
Debra Weatherley
Production: Viv Hichens

Originated by Dot Gradations Limited
Printed in China by WKT Company Limited

ISBN 0 431 17835 6 (hardback)
08 07 06 05 04
10 9 8 7 6 5 4 3 2 1

ISBN 0 431 17863 1 (paperback)
09 08 07 06 05
10 9 8 7 6 5 4 3 2 1

British Library Cataloguing in Publication Data

Spilsbury, Richard, 1963 –
Howling hurricanes. – (Awesome forces
of nature)
1. Hurricanes – Juvenile literature
I. Title II. Spilsbury, Louise
551.5′52
A full catalogue record for this book is
available from the British Library.

Acknowledgements

The publishers would like to thank the
following for permission to reproduce
photographs:

Associated Press pp. **13** (Jose Goitia), **20**
(John McConnico), **23** (Victor Caivano), **26**
(Bob Coates), **28**; Corbis/Bettmann pp. **10**,
24; Getty News and Sport p. **14**; NASA
p. **25**; NOAA pp. **5** (Fema), **19**, **21**; Panos
p. **6** (Bruce Paton); Reuters pp. **9**, **15**, **27**;
Rex Features pp. **16** (Peter Heismath), **17**
(Sipa); Science Photo Library pp. **7**, **18**
(NASA/Goddard Space Flight Centre); Still
Pictures p. **22** (Julio Etchart); Trip pp. **4**
(Viesti Collection), **8** (NASA).

Cover photograph reproduced courtesy of
Reuters/Jorge Silva.

Every effort has been made to contact
copyright holders of any material
reproduced in this book. Any omissions will
be rectified in subsequent printings if notice
is given to the publishers.

Contents

*Any words appearing in the text in bold, **like this**, are explained in the Glossary.*

What is a hurricane?

Hurricanes are the most powerful storms on Earth. They grow from **tropical** storms over the sea. Some stay over the open ocean, far from land, and some weaken and die out before they reach land. Others hurtle towards a shore at high speed.

Hurricane winds often travel at speeds of up to 350 kilometres per hour – faster than the quickest train on Earth! If hurricanes reach land, their violent, fast winds and heavy rain can cause terrible damage and destruction. Some only last for days, others can go on for weeks. Hurricanes usually cause most damage around coasts, but big hurricanes can sometimes reach far inland.

These waves are being whipped up by a Caribbean hurricane. The word 'hurricane' is said to come from the name of a god of evil, 'Hurican'. People in the Caribbean in the past gave it this name because of its destructive power.

Hurricanes cause great destruction when they move onto land. They can blow down buildings, pull up trees and throw cars and boats around like toys. They also whip up the sea to form giant waves that crash onto shores. Heavy rains can cause floods, when land that is normally dry is covered in water. In the past, hurricanes killed many people. Today **scientists** usually spot dangerous hurricanes early and warn people to move to a safe place.

Naming hurricanes

Scientists give hurricanes boys' and girls' names. They do this so that everyone who talks about a particular hurricane, whether they are scientists or ordinary people, know which one it is. The names go in alphabetical order, but scientists don't use Q, U, X, Y or Z as there are few names starting with these letters.

This is just some of the damage caused by Hurricane Camille, which hit the USA in August 1969.

How do hurricanes happen?

Hurricanes always begin over warm water. Warm water heats up the air just above it. When air heats up, it becomes lighter and it rises up higher in the sky. When the layer of warm air moves up, cooler air fills the space it has left. This causes winds.

Over **tropical** waters that reach very high temperatures, the heat makes the air rise very quickly. As the winds and clouds rise, they move faster and faster. They also start to **rotate** in a spiral. When the winds in this spinning storm reach about 120 kilometres per hour, it is called a hurricane. The whirling pattern of the winds makes the air inside the hurricane move even faster.

Hurricanes may begin like this – as winds that merely whip up waves on the sea. A hurricane usually takes days to develop. The fastest a hurricane might form is two days.

How do hurricanes die?

Hurricanes are created and powered by the heat that comes off very warm water. As hurricanes move over land which is cooler than the sea, or over cooler stretches of water, they weaken and start to die out. A hurricane without warm water is like a toy car with a run-down battery – it gradually loses power and then stops altogether.

Top hurricane speeds

No one really knows exactly how fast the fastest hurricanes go because measuring equipment is often destroyed by the hurricane. Some **scientists** believe that the fastest hurricane winds are around 300 kilometres an hour, while others say they might reach almost 600 kilometres per hour!

If fast enough, winds above a warm sea can start spinning within 12 hours. You can see the winds spiralling fast in this picture from above a hurricane, taken from the Space Shuttle.

What is a hurricane's eye?

The **eye** of a hurricane is at its centre, inside the swirling mass of wind and cloud. If you could fly high above a hurricane and look down inside it, it would look like water spinning out of a plughole. The centre is calm and the strongest winds spin around it in the **eyewall**. When the eye passes over land, people below feel just a gentle breeze and the rain stops. As the hurricane moves on, the winds at the edge of the eye – the eyewall – begin again.

Making a mini-hurricane eye

You can create your own mini-hurricane eye after a bath. When the water spirals around the plug hole, right in the middle there is a dry centre. This is just like the eye of a hurricane, except that in a hurricane you get huge spiralling winds and clouds instead of swirling water.

This photo was taken directly over the eye of a hurricane. Most hurricanes have an eye between 30–60 kilometres (18–37 miles) across.

How do hurricane rains form?

Hurricanes almost always bring very heavy rains. Hurricanes do this because as they travel across oceans they suck water up into the sky. They do this by a process called **evaporation**. Evaporation happens when water warms up to a certain temperature. Then it stops being a liquid and it turns into a gas in the air, called water vapour. This is how wet clothes dry outside after washing. The water inside them is warmed by the air and evaporates, leaving the clothes dry.

Water vapour turns back into water when it cools down. Hurricane winds cool down when they get nearer land and further away from the warm oceans. This is when the vapour they are carrying turns back into liquid. It falls from the sky as heavy rain.

Large hurricanes can carry vast amounts of water vapour. This means that they can cause incredibly heavy rainstorms, like this one during Hurricane Keith, which hit Belize in October 2000.

Where do hurricanes happen?

Hurricanes only start over really warm water, so they only form in certain parts of the world. Hurricanes never start over cold oceans, such as the South Atlantic. They form over **tropical** oceans. These areas of water are near the **Equator**, an imaginary line around the centre of the Earth, where it is always very warm.

When is a hurricane not a hurricane?

Hurricanes are called different names in different parts of the world. These storms are called hurricanes when they happen over the North Atlantic and Northeast Pacific oceans. When they occur in the Pacific and Indian Oceans they are called typhoons or cyclones. Even though they have different names, they are the same kind of storm.

This picture shows some of the destruction caused by Cyclone Tracy in Darwin, Australia in 1974. Cyclones and typhoons are the same kind of storms as hurricanes, but they have different names because they start in different parts of the world.

Hurricanes on the move

Once a storm has started, it does not stay in one place. Hurricanes can travel thousands of kilometres over the oceans. They move like a spinning top – spiralling around their **eye** at high speeds. At the same time, the whole storm moves slowly forwards or backwards in another direction. Most hurricanes travel generally west or northwards. The average speed for a hurricane to travel is 10 kilometres an hour.

Hurricanes occur in the **northern hemisphere** and cyclones happen mostly in the **southern hemisphere**. Hurricanes and cyclones usually spin in opposite directions. This is because the Earth is turning slowly all the time. As it turns, it pulls the winds blowing above its surface in different directions. It pulls winds to the right in the northern hemisphere and to the left in the southern hemisphere. This means hurricanes spin anticlockwise and cyclones spin clockwise!

The arrows on this world map show where hurricanes, cyclones and typhoons usually form and the routes that they usually take.

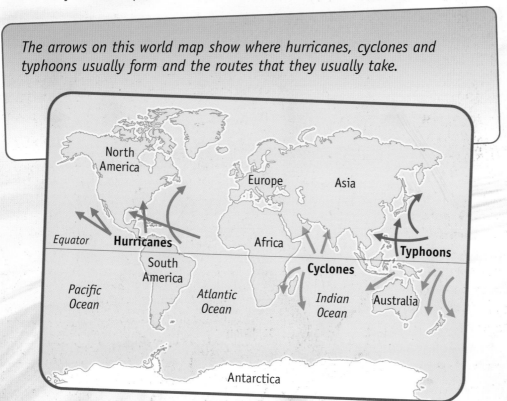

When do hurricanes happen?

Hurricanes happen every year. There has been a hurricane, cyclone or typhoon recorded every year for the past 500 years. It is likely that they happened just as regularly before that, too. Every year there is also at least one major hurricane which reaches land somewhere and causes damage or destruction.

Hurricanes always happen at certain times of the year, known as the **hurricane seasons**. In tropical oceans and seas, like the Gulf of Mexico and the Caribbean Sea, the hurricane season begins in May or June. In the Atlantic Ocean they usually happen from July to October. Hurricane seasons may last up to six months, but the worst storms usually happen over a two-month period – for example, July and August in the eastern Pacific.

This graph shows the number of hurricanes that have happened at certain times of year over the past century in the Atlantic Ocean, the Caribbean Sea and the Gulf of Mexico. As you can see, the peak of the hurricane season is from mid-August to late October.

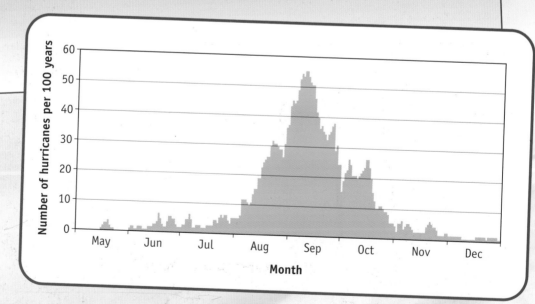

Hurricanes Isidore and Lili, Cuba, 2002

In a **hurricane season**, hurricanes can sometimes strike one after another. In 2002 Hurricane Isidore hit Cuba on 20 September, followed less than two weeks later by Hurricane Lili. Even though most people moved to a safe place before the hurricanes hit, many thousands of houses were damaged or destroyed. The hurricanes also reached Louisiana and Texas on the south-east coast of the USA. By the time they got there they were weaker, but they still caused serious damage.

'Some fishing villages were wiped off the map. People could not take anything with them, so when they returned to their homes everything they had was destroyed.' Cristina Estrada, a worker for the Red Cross, an **aid organization** that helps people in emergencies

Isidore and Lili were strong hurricanes, with winds up to 200 kilometres per hour. The winds battered the coasts, ripping up trees and damaging buildings.

What happens in a hurricane?

As a hurricane passes directly over people or places, there are three different stages. First, wind builds up, becoming very fast and bringing heavy rain. Then the wind dies down and the rain stops. This is when the calm centre – the **eye** – of the hurricane passes over. This can last for minutes or even hours, as hurricanes sometimes hover over one place. Then, it moves on and the other side of the hurricane passes over, bringing more fierce winds from the opposite direction and rain.

Hurricanes bring heavy showers of rain. These can cause flooding on land. A hurricane's high winds can whip up high waves that crash onto shores. Hurricanes can also cause **tornadoes**.

Many people have died after going outside while the eye of the storm was passing over, because they thought the hurricane was over. To be safe, people should stay in shelters like this one until the storm is completely over.

Tornadoes

Tornadoes can form in thunderstorms and hurricanes. A tornado is a tall funnel of wind that spins very fast. Tornadoes look like a rope of cloud coming down from a storm cloud. They are smaller and even faster than hurricane winds. Unlike hurricanes, tornadoes can travel far across land. This means they pass over more places where people live, causing lots of damage.

What damage do hurricane winds cause?

Hurricane winds are so fast and strong they can move large objects as easily as blowing a hat off your head. Even the weakest hurricane winds can blow tiles off roofs, rattle windows and snap branches. The worst hurricanes can blow down trees and move cars and **mobile homes**.

Strong hurricane winds often knock down electricity and telephone cables. This means people cannot use electric lights or cookers and may not be able to call others for help.

Rain damage

Hurricanes can drop huge amounts of rain over a short period of time. A big hurricane can drop so much rain that it causes floods. Floods are when land that is usually dry becomes covered with water. This can happen when rainwater makes rivers so high that the water spills over the sides and onto the land around it.

When floodwater sweeps through a town or city it can damage buildings and bury houses under mud. It drowns people if they cannot get away in time. When floodwater covers fields of crops it ruins them and it can also drown farm animals. When this happens it can leave people dangerously short of food.

In 1996, Hurricane Fran dropped huge amounts of rain in Alexandria, Virginia, USA. This heavy rainfall caused serious floods across the region.

What is a storm surge?

When a hurricane gets close to land, the winds can push a high wall of water in front of them. This is called a **storm surge**. When this kind of wave hits land it can cause terrible damage to the coastline.

Storm surges can change the whole shape of the land. They may destroy beaches by dragging the sand and rocks out to sea. Sometimes they dump sand and create new beaches. Finally, storm surges can also cover land and cause floods.

HURRICANE ⚡ FACTS

These are things that people should do in a hurricane:

! Stay indoors and keep away from windows.

! If electricity is cut off, use torches to see in the dark. Do not use candles, which can cause fires if they are blown over.

! Listen to radio or TV reports and take the advice given by experts and emergency services.

The combination of winds, rain and storm surges causes terrible damage. In 1996, Hurricane Fran ruined thousands of homes and flattened millions of trees up to 240 kilometres inland from the sea in North Carolina, USA.

Hurricane Andrew, USA, 1992

The first hurricane in the US **hurricane season** of 1992 arrived in southern Florida on 24 August. It was named Hurricane Andrew. Hurricane Andrew's winds were spiralling at about 280 kilometres per hour and it was travelling across land at about 30 kilometres per hour. As it moved over the warm waters of the Gulf of Mexico it gained strength. It only began to weaken as it travelled over land across the state of Louisiana. Hurricane Andrew caused over 60 deaths and huge amounts of damage.

'I've lived through ten hurricanes in my lifetime, and this is going to be the worst. I'm scared. I won't lie to you. I am scared.'
Louisiana cafe worker, Janice Semien

This special picture, taken over a period of four days, shows the movements of Hurricane Andrew between 23 and 26 August 1992.

What damage did Hurricane Andrew cause?

Andrew turned out to be one of America's most expensive hurricanes. Out at sea it churned up high waves, which toppled **oil platforms** and badly damaged **oil wells**. When it passed over coastlines, **storm surges** smashed millions of dollars' worth of boats and ships moored in the water.

Scientists who were following the movements of the hurricane were able to warn people it was coming. About 2 million people were **evacuated** – they left their homes to stay somewhere safer. The hurricane damaged or destroyed houses, **mobile homes**, businesses, bridges and roads. It also badly damaged the Louisiana fishing industry. Over 184 million fish were killed in one area alone!

The buildings and many other structures that Hurricane Andrew damaged or destroyed cost over 20 billion US dollars to mend or rebuild.

Who helps after a hurricane?

After a hurricane has passed over, the danger does not end. Most people who die because of a hurricane drown in floods. Emergency service workers, such as fire rescue workers and the **armed forces**, get people to a safe place.

Other workers, from local hospitals and **aid organizations** like the Red Cross, set up first-aid stations to treat wounds. They also set up shelters where people who have been **evacuated** from their homes can stay. They give **evacuees** blankets, water, food and any medical supplies they need. Emergency workers travel around the area to fix fallen electric power lines that could **electrocute** people, and cut down damaged trees that could fall on them.

Sometimes rescue workers have to lift people out of dangerous fast-flowing flood water caused by hurricanes. This baby was rescued from floods caused by Hurricane Hortense in Puerto Rico in September 1996.

Rich and poor

It takes time to put things back to normal after a hurricane. Bridges and buildings have to be rebuilt or mended. Water companies mend broken **sewage** and water pipes. Government workers clean roads of obstructions such as mud, broken branches and wrecked signs. Generally, people in rich, **developed countries** recover fairly quickly.

In a **developing country**, flooding from a hurricane can cause more long-term suffering. Poorer families usually do not have **insurance** or savings to pay for repairs. If their **crops** are ruined, they may starve. Aid organizations, such as Oxfam, and the governments of other countries send help. They may supply farm equipment, seeds and farm animals. They may also send building equipment, so that people can rebuild their homes themselves.

*Charities make sure that **aid** such as clean water supplies gets to the people who need it most after a hurricane.*

Hurricane Mitch, Central America, 1998

In October 1998 a terrible hurricane raged across Central America. Winds up to 250 kilometres per hour swept through, bringing torrential rains. Hurricane Mitch left over 9000 people dead, many missing and millions more people without homes. Roads and bridges were wrecked by the storm. Floods ruined farmland, many **crops** and people's food stores. Heavy rains caused **landslides** too. A landslide is when mud and rock slide down a hill causing great damage.

'Some neighbourhoods were flooded by water up to 1.5 metres high. People screamed asking for help and some of us, helped by tyre inner-tubes, threw ourselves in [the water] to rescue those trapped in their homes.' Roberto Ramos, a Honduran nurse

Many people in Central America work on banana plantations (farms) like this. Hurricane Mitch destroyed most of the country's banana plants. This meant that many people lost their jobs and their chance of earning money to look after their families.

GUATEMALA

HONDURAS

EL SALVADOR

NICARAGUA

KEY
— Mitch

Long-term support

At first, **aid organizations** such as Oxfam and the Red Cross helped by giving people food, water, medical treatment and somewhere to stay. They also helped people find family members who got lost in all the chaos.

Later their main aim was to get farms working again. That way people could feed themselves, without having to rely on help from other people. **Aid** organizations worked with local groups to plan what to do. Gradually, they helped people grow new corn, rice, bean and banana plants to eat and sell. The poorest people in the area were the worst affected. Their houses were flimsy and had been completely wrecked by the hurricane. Aid organizations helped people build new, stronger homes, as well as new wells, bridges and roads.

Many banana plantations had to be replanted with baby banana plants after the entire crop was destroyed by Hurricane Mitch.

Can hurricanes be predicted?

Predicting hurricanes is difficult because each one grows and moves differently. Some countries spend a lot of money on **scientists** and equipment to try to work out when and where hurricanes might happen. If they can work out where a hurricane is heading, they can tell people in that area to **evacuate**.

Satellite pictures

Weather **satellites** are special computers that are sent out into space. From space they photograph the clouds high above the Earth. This helps scientists on Earth to predict the weather. Hurricane experts study these pictures to see if there are any clouds that look like they could become hurricanes. They also use powerful supercomputers. These examine weather and hurricane information from around the world to help them with their predictions.

These scientists at the US National Hurricane Center are using a computer-enhanced satellite photo to track the progress of a hurricane as it approaches the USA.

Hurricane hunters

When dangerous-looking storm clouds are spotted, hurricane hunters go to look at them. These people fly planes all around and into storms and hurricanes. They have special equipment to take measurements and pictures of the weather inside the storm.

For example, they drop miniature weather stations into a hurricane's **eyewall** on a parachute. This measures things like temperature, **humidity** and wind speed. It sends the information to experts' computers. The experts look at this information along with satellite pictures and facts about the way that hurricanes in the past grew. This helps them to work out how strong a hurricane is and which way it is likely to go.

*The hurricane hunters in this plane are part of the United States Air Force. Hurricane hunters are skilled pilots who fly right into the **eyes** of storms and hurricanes. They may stay in the air for up to fourteen hours at a time!*

Can people prepare for hurricanes?

When **scientists** predict a hurricane, they send out warnings on TV and radio. If it is a very dangerous hurricane this gives people time to **evacuate**. If it is a weaker hurricane this gives people time to prepare for the storm. Most people who live in areas where there is a danger of hurricanes make some preparations in advance.

Long-term preparations

People can do several things to make their houses safer. For example, they can fix strong shutters to their windows. When these are closed, they stop hurricane winds shattering the glass. People also cut down dead branches or trees. In hurricanes these can cause a lot of damage when they snap off and blow about.

*Before a **hurricane season**, some governments advise people to stock up on essential supplies. Items include tinned foods, batteries for torches and portable radios, bottled water and a first-aid kit.*

Governments can prepare for hurricanes further ahead, when planning new structures such as buildings and bridges. They can make stronger buildings that can cope with strong wind and rain. They can put important buildings, such as hospitals, further inland where they are safer from hurricanes. They can also build bigger storm drains that allow large amounts of water to soak away. This means that future floods will not be so deep.

HURRICANE ⚡ FACTS

If a hurricane is on its way, but not one strong enough that people need to evacuate, there are still a number of steps that they should take:

- People should check their portable radio has batteries.

- They should bring in or tie down loose objects outside, such as garden furniture.

- They should close windows and shutters.

- They should move food and other supplies into the basement or cellar (or the lowest room of the house) where people will be during the storm.

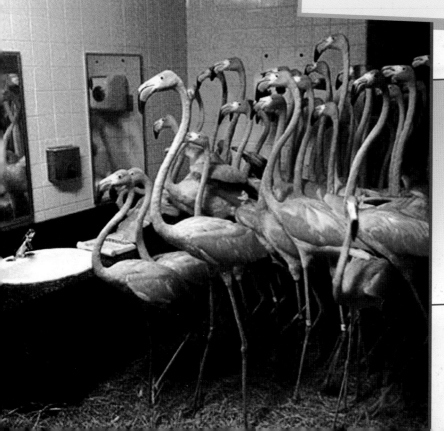

It is important that all animals are safe inside too. These flamingos from Miami Zoo, USA, are sheltering from a hurricane in one of the zoo toilets!

Can hurricanes be prevented?

People have tried to prevent hurricanes in the past. In 1947, **scientists** tried to weaken a hurricane over water near America. They flew planes into the storm and dropped dry ice into the clouds to try to cool and calm it before it reached the shore. It did not work! Scientists today are working on new ideas, but we may never be able to stop hurricanes.

Scientists have learned a great deal about how hurricanes work. This is important, especially when more and more people are building homes near coastlines. Although it is impossible to predict all hurricanes, tracking and warning systems can help to save lives. They give people time to escape and lessen the damage these awesome forces of nature can cause.

In 1935 a hurricane hit Florida Keys, USA, killing around 408 people. In 1960 Hurricane Donna (right) hit the same area. Even though many more people were living there, early warnings meant that only three people died this time.

Howling hurricanes of the past

1900, Galveston Hurricane
Storm-surge waves 4.5 metres high swamped the whole of Galveston city and parts of the Texas coast in the USA. Around 8000 people died.

1926, Great Miami Hurricane
This storm caused over 100 million US dollars of damage in Florida, USA. If the same storm were to happen today it would cause 80 billion US dollars of damage because there are so many more people living in Florida now!

1944, Great Atlantic Hurricane
This major hurricane hit the eastern US coast. Over 20 centimetres of rain and 200-kilometre-per-hour winds caused 46 deaths.

1969, Hurricane Camille
Huge floods struck after as much as 70 centimetres of rain fell in 5 hours when this hurricane hit the Mississippi Gulf Coast, USA, killing 250 people.

1974, Cyclone Tracy
This hurricane hit Darwin, Australia, on Christmas Day morning, 1974. A total of 50 people were killed and 112 more were seriously injured. Around 90 per cent of the city was damaged.

1974, Hurricane Fifi
This hurricane devastated large areas of Honduras in Central America. Over 60,000 people were left homeless and 8000 died.

1979, Hurricane David
This hurricane caused over 1 billion US dollars' worth of damage to Dominica and the Dominican Republic in the Caribbean.

1979, Typhoon Tip
This awesome typhoon was at least 1000 kilometres across, with wind speeds over 300 kilometres per hour. Luckily, Typhoon Tip never directly hit land.

1984, Typhoon Ike
Over a million people were made homeless after Typhoon Ike hit the Philippines.

Glossary

aid help given as money, medicine, food or other essential items

aid organizations groups that raise money and provide help for people in need

armed forces army, air force and navy. These forces have equipment to fight with but also help rescue people at other times.

crops plants grown to eat and to sell, such as rice and bananas

developed countries richer countries of the world that have well-developed services for their people, such as good hospitals and emergency services

developing countries poorer countries of the world that are gradually developing better conditions for their people

electrocute injure or kill with electricity

Equator imaginary line around the centre of the Earth

evacuate when people move from a dangerous place to somewhere safe

evacuee someone who moves from a dangerous place to somewhere safe

evaporate when water turns from liquid into a vapour (a gas in the air)

eye calm centre of a hurricane

eyewall edge of the eye of a hurricane

humidity when the weather is very warm and moist at the same time

hurricane season some areas have hurricanes every year at about the same time. This is called the hurricane season.

insurance when people pay money regularly to a company that pays the full cost of rebuilding their home or business if it is damaged or destroyed

landslides when heavy rains and wind make large amounts of mud and rock slide down a hill or mountain

mobile home home that can be moved using lorries. Most mobile homes look a bit like big caravans without wheels.

northern hemisphere everywhere on the Earth north of the Equator

oil platform/well an oil platform is a building at sea around an oil well. An oil well is a deep narrow hole drilled to release oil found underground.

rotate spin or turn around

satellite object in space that sends out TV signals or takes photographs

scientists people who study aspects of the world around us

sewage waste from lavatories

southern hemisphere everywhere on the Earth south of the Equator

storm surge when the sea becomes high along a coast due to storm winds

tornadoes strong whirlwinds that move quickly over land

tropical in the tropics – regions around the Equator that have hot and humid weather

Find out more

Books

DK Eyewitness Guides: Hurricane and Tornado, Jack Challoner (Dorling Kindersley, 2000)

DK Guide to Weather, Michael Allaby (Dorling Kindersley, 2000)

Hurricanes and Tornadoes, Neil Morris (Crabtree Pub Co., 1998)

Natural Disasters: Hurricanes and Typhoons, J. Dineen (Franklin Watts, 2002)

Storms, Mark Maslin (Hodder Children's Books, 2000)

Wild Weather: Thunderstorm, Catherine Chambers (Heinemann Library, 2002)

Websites

www.howstuffworks.com/hurricane.htm – to find out more about how hurricanes work go to the hurricane pages.

www.nhc.noaa.gov – read up about America's national hurricane centre if you want to know more about tracking hurricanes.

www.fema.gov/hazards/hurricanes – for facts about hurricane dangers, what to do and how to prepare.

Disclaimer
All the Internet addresses (URLs) given in this book were valid at the time of going to press. However, due to the dynamic nature of the Internet, some addresses may have changed, or sites may have changed or ceased to exist since publication. While the author and publishers regret any inconvenience this may cause readers, no responsibility for any such changes can be accepted by either the author or the publishers.

Index